Coaching Skills
*A Guide
for Supervisors*

Coaching Skills
A Guide for Supervisors

ROBERT W. LUCAS

The Business Skills Express Series

McGraw-Hill ·

New York San Francisco Washington, D.C. Auckland Bogotá Caracas
Lisbon London Madrid Mexico City Milan Montreal New Delhi
San Juan Singapore Sydney Tokyo Toronto

McGraw-Hill

A Division of The McGraw·Hill Companies

This publication is designed to provide accurate and
authoritative information in regard to the subject matter
covered. It is sold with the understanding that neither the
author nor the publisher is engaged in rendering legal, accounting,
or other professional service. If legal advice or other expert
assistance is required, the services of a competent
professional person should be sought.

*From a Declaration of Principles jointly adopted by a Committee
of the American Bar Association and a Committee of Publishers.*

Mirror Press:	David R. Helmstadter
	Carla F. Tishler
Editor-in-chief:	Jeffrey A. Krames
Marketing manager:	Lynn M. Kalanik
Project editor:	Lynne Basler
Production manager:	Jon Christopher
Art manager:	Kim Meriwether
Compositor:	Alexander Graphics, Inc.
Typeface:	12/14 Criterion
Printer:	Malloy Lithographing, Inc.

Library of Congress Cataloging-in-Publication Data

Lucas, Robert W.
    Coaching skills : a guide for supervisors / Robert W. Lucas.
      p.   cm.—(Business skills express series)
     ISBN 0-7863-0220-8
     1. Supervision of employees. I. Title. II. Series
     HF5549.12.L83   1994
     658.3'1244—dc20   93–44766

Printed in the United States of America
  6 7 8 9 MAL/MAL 9 0 2 1

PREFACE

The world of business and industry is evolving at an unprecedented rate. As international competition, technology, and shifts in socioeconomic structure all hit organizations simultaneously, change becomes essential to success. The ultimate impact of change usually falls on the shoulders of frontline workers and their supervisors. What does this mean for supervisors? A lot! Changing workplace rules make it necessary to modify basic beliefs, systems, and actions within organizations. Since much of this burden does fall on the shoulders of supervisors, they must, now more than ever, learn to communicate with employees and coach their performance.

In reading and using the information and examples in this book, you will gain valuable insights and strategies to improve your effectiveness. Each chapter starts with a scenario based on situations encountered by supervisors every day. Think about these situations before reading the chapter text to help focus your attention. Once you have completed the material review, develop an action plan to use in your workplace.

This book provides opportunities for assessing your knowledge of coaching by exploring new ideas and reviewing key skills you may or may not have already mastered. Checkpoints at the end of each chapter solidify the concepts. When you complete the book, you will be able to:

- Explain the need for coaching in a variety of organizational settings.
- List a variety of situations where coaching can be effective.
- Apply strategies to improve interpersonal communication in the workplace.
- Implement techniques to improve your success when giving and receiving performance feedback.
- Define the steps of an effective coaching model that can be used in hierarchical and team-driven environments.
- Execute strategies for dealing both with substandard performers and with superstars.

- Identify approaches for coaching employees with disabilities and complying with the Americans with Disabilities Act of 1990.
- Develop or improve a system for accurately documenting all employee coaching activities.

As with any other initiative, you will get out of this book what you put into it. Absorb the techniques, strategies, and ideas you find in *Coaching Skills: A Guide for Supervisors,* then go out and put them into practice. You and your employees will be glad you did.

Robert W. Lucas

ABOUT THE AUTHOR

Robert William Lucas is the training manager at the national headquarters of the American Automobile Association in Heathrow, Florida. He has extensive experience in the training, development, and management fields. For the past 20 years, he has conducted training in profit, nonprofit, not-for-profit, military, government, consulting, and volunteer environments. His areas of expertise include management and training program development, interpersonal communication, adult learning, customer service and employee development. Bob has served on the board of directors for the Metropolitan Chapter of the American Society for Training and Development in Washington, D.C., and in Orlando, Florida, where he is currently president-elect. Additionally, Bob is the national ASTD codirector for the Associations and Non-Profit Industry Group, has given presentations to various local and national groups and organizations, serves on a variety of product advisory committees for several national organizations, is on the curriculum review board of Orlando College, and is an adjunct faculty member at several Orlando area colleges.

About the Business Skills Express Series

This expanding series of authoritative, concise, and fast-paced books delivers high-quality training on key business topics at a remarkably affordable cost. The series will help managers, supervisors, and frontline personnel in organizations of all sizes and types hone their business skills while enhancing job performance and career satisfaction.

Business Skills Express books are ideal for employee seminars, independent self-study, on-the-job training, and classroom-based instruction. Express books are also convenient-to-use references at work.

CONTENTS

Self-Assessment

We all have an image of how well we perform in various areas of our lives. As a leader, you must know your skill levels for communicating with and coaching others in the workplace. To help give you an idea of how well you currently perform in these areas, take a few minutes to rate the following statements, using the key below. Each statement focuses on characteristics commonly exhibited by successful performance coaches. Rate yourself as you believe your employees or co-workers would rate you. The results will help you to focus on specific information as you read.

Note: Since your image of yourself often differs from the one others have of you, make copies of this survey before completing it. Once you have rated yourself, distribute copies to your employees and co-workers familiar with your coaching style and ask them to rate you. Compare all the results and develop an action plan to improve your skills.

Select the number that best defines your behavior when coaching.

	(1) Rarely	(2) Some-times	(3) Fre-quently	(4) Usually	(5) Always
1. I give all necessary details when assigning tasks.	___	___	___	___	___
2. I provide an environment in which win-win relationships are common.	___	___	___	___	___
3. I strive to develop employees to their fullest potential.	___	___	___	___	___
4. I provide frequent, specific performance feedback to employees.	___	___	___	___	___
5. I work with employees to develop measurable and attainable goals.	___	___	___	___	___
6. I actively solicit, listen to, and follow up on employee suggestions.	___	___	___	___	___
7. I explain the reasons for my decisions that affect employees.	___	___	___	___	___
8. I encourage employees to be creative in problem solving.	___	___	___	___	___

	(1) Rarely	(2) Some- times	(3) Fre- quently	(4) Usually	(5) Always
9. I applaud employee successes in a manner appropriate to the situation and the individual employee.	_____	_____	_____	_____	_____
10. When employees are not totally successful in their performance efforts, I give constructive criticism, suggesting potential corrective actions.	_____	_____	_____	_____	_____

Scoring: Total up all the points you have given yourself.

45–50: You have excellent coaching skills. This book will help you to maintain the coaching skills you have as well as provide some insights that may be new to you.

40–44: You are doing a good job coaching. This book will help you to keep the skills you have in shape as well as teach you some new ones to increase your effectiveness.

30–39: You presently are trying to be a good coach but you need help staying focused. This book will provide you with material you can use to improve on the job you are doing.

20–29: Your coaching skills need improvement. This book will help you learn the importance of being a good coach, and it will give you the tools you need to become one.

Below 20: Your coaching style needs serious reevaluation. This book will provide you with the information and skills necessary to become a good coach.

1 | Why Coach?

This chapter will help you to:

- Define performance coaching.
- Describe the characteristics of an effective coach.
- Explain the importance of coaching in improving workplace effectiveness.
- Identify and eliminate excuses for not coaching.

Cynthia Harding is a talented and enthusiastic recent college graduate. Nine months ago she joined Theresa Jackson's department at OralTech, Inc., to fill a newly created marketing position. Because of the organization's stellar reputation in the community and what Cynthia has heard of the environment at the company, her expectations of success are high.

From her first contact with Theresa, Cynthia had a feeling that she had made the right choice in coming to work at OralTech. Theresa has spent hours explaining policies, procedures, and systems. She goes out of her way daily to say good morning and to give constant feedback to all of her employees.

Recently, Cynthia completed a proposal that has the potential of improving the marketing process and increasing sales for a major product line. If projections are correct, the company could make hundreds of thousands of dollars in additional revenue annually. In recognition of Cynthia's accomplishment, Theresa wrote a letter of appreciation that was presented at the monthly staff meeting. She also submitted Cynthia's name for consideration to receive the company's Superior Performance award. ■

1

Questions to Consider

1. What role do you think Theresa has played in helping Cynthia meet her goals? Why?

_____

_____

_____

2. What type of positive coaching activities are evident in this scenario?

_____

_____

_____

Any time an employee joins an organization, the supervisor must begin coaching. Lack of coaching often results in frustration for the employee *and* the supervisor.

SHIFTS IN SUPERVISORY BEHAVIOR

In many organizations, supervisory roles and behavior are changing to match new demands. This is especially so in organizations that have moved from a hierarchical structure to a team structure. These structural shifts may include the following moves:

From ⟶	To
Directing	Guiding
Dictating	Participating
Delegating	Empowering
Telling	Listening
Planning	Consulting
Competing	Cooperating
Nonrisk taking	Risk taking
Focusing on bottom line	Focusing on people

Have you observed other changes in your organization?

No matter what the environment, a supervisor's success depends on the ability to work effectively through people. Similarly, employees' abilities to function productively, grow personally, and expand professionally depend on the support and encouragement of their supervisors. An effective supervisor creates an environment where one-on-one communication, effective listening, empathy, compassionate problem solving, and mentoring are common.

WHAT IS COACHING?

If you are like most supervisors, you probably coach all the time. Coaching is a simple process used to develop employees through ongoing one-on-one communication. In the process of coaching, supervisors and employees jointly strive to identify, develop, and reach performance goals. If done correctly, the results are beneficial to the organization, the supervisor, and the employees. When supervisors fail to use coaching effectively and continuously, the employee/supervisor relationship becomes laborious and dysfunctional. In fact, one of the key reasons for high turnover, disciplinary and performance problems, and supervisor failure is the lack of a functional coaching system.

What Does Coaching Involve?

Any activity in which the supervisor and employee work toward employee performance improvement can be categorized as coaching. Here are a few skills used in coaching:

- Instructing.
- Communicating.
- Analyzing.
- Training.
- Facilitating.
- Directing.
- Delegating.
- Assisting.
- Collaborating.
- Guiding.
- Motivating.
- Nurturing.
- Supporting.

1

■ **Personal Reflection**

Take a few minutes to think about how you have seen these traits in action by picturing someone who demonstrates some or all of these coaching skills:

- Who was the person and what was his or her position or role(s)?

  _____

  _____

- What did he or she do that makes him or her stand out in your mind as an excellent coach?

  _____

  _____

- Exactly which characteristics did he or she exhibit on a regular basis?

  _____

  _____

- Even though this person exemplified coaching effectiveness in your mind, is there anything he or she could have done better to guide protégés?

  _____

  _____

As you continue through this book, keep this coach in mind.

CHARACTERISTICS OF AN EFFECTIVE COACH

Certain traits characterize a good coach. These include:

- Excellent communication skills (verbal and written).
- Excellent listening skills.
- Compassion.
- Technical proficiency.
- Enthusiasm.
- Ability to organize.
- Flexibility.
- Receptivity to feedback.
- Nurturing disposition.

1

- Goal orientation.
- People orientation.
- Creativity.
- Team-player mentality.

What other qualities do you feel are important in a good coach? Consider good coaches that you have known in various situations outside the workplace, such as schools, sports, scouts, church, committees, and so on.

BENEFITS OF COACHING

Think about all the benefits that can be gained from effectively coaching employees. If you are like most supervisors, you can probably come up with quite a few. Take a look at a few of the more common benefits:

1. *Reduced costs and turnover.* Unhappy employees often leave an organization only after they have caused severe morale and productivity problems. One disgruntled employee can create havoc among fellow employees, especially if the departing employee has been the work unit's informal leader.

2. *Improved quality and quantity of work.* By helping develop employee knowledge, skills, and attitudes, the supervisor can enhance the overall effectiveness of both the employee and the organization.

3. *Enhanced employee growth.* Through an ongoing process of imparting up-to-date information, role modeling, and demonstrating support, supervisors can function as valuable resources for employees.

4. *Improved employee problem-solving ability.* A primary goal of any supervisor should be to develop individual employees to the point where they can assume the supervisor's job. By doing this, the supervisor becomes known as a strong leader and increases his or her own promotion potential while making the employees a more valuable resource within the work unit.

5. *Increased likelihood that goals will be reached.* For employees to attain the goals that you have set with them, they need continuing feedback and reinforcement. Supervisors who assume that employees know how well (or poorly) they are doing in goal attainment are setting up a situation for failure. By communicating regularly, supervisors stay abreast of employee progress and head off potential problems before situations get out of control.

6. *Enriched transfer of training.* It is estimated that U.S. organizations spend approximately $210 billion annually on employee training. Unfortunately, many of these dollars are lost because supervisory personnel do not set up a learning environment to reinforce key elements of any training received. To maximize return on investment, you should take the following steps:

- Before an employee attends a training session, sit down to discuss any employees knowledge, skill, or attitude deficits.
- Select a training program with objectives, information, materials, and activities that address the employee's needs.
- Discuss with the employee specific issues or information that should be the focus of the training.
- Immediately following the training, schedule time to sit down again with the employee to review key elements of the training.
- As part of the post-session review, jointly develop an action plan with the employee to implement what was learned in training.
- Schedule additional dates to reinforce and review progress.
- Include comments concerning pre- and post-training performance on the employee's performance appraisal.

7. *Improved supervisor/employee communication.* By sitting down and talking together on a regular basis, employees and supervisors can share expectations and reduce misunderstandings.

EXCUSES FOR FAILING TO COACH

With all the potential benefits that coaching can offer, why don't supervisors do more of it? They have excuses. Here are some of the more commonly given reasons for *not* coaching employees:

1. *It takes too long.* True, coaching does take an investment of time on the part of the supervisor and the employee. The question is, "Do I have time later to fix problems because the employee didn't have the information, tools, or proper attitude to perform?"

2. *If employees need help, they'll ask.* Although many people are not reluctant to ask for information and assistance, some employees are.

3. *I don't know how.* Supervisors often fall back on this excuse. As with any other supervisory skill, you will have to learn coaching skills through training or from a qualified mentor who can teach you.

4. *Employees might think I don't trust them.* Part of your job is to ensure that employees complete tasks effectively and efficiently. If you never talk to them, you will never know how they are doing. The key to effective coaching is to let your employees know your expectations as soon as they join your team. Discussing your management style and goals up front can eliminate potential misunderstandings later.

5. *I've got other more important things to do.* Your success as a supervisor *depends* on your ability to work through your people. If employees do not get the guidance and support they need to be successful, then you will also fail.

6. *It's the trainer's job to teach skills.* Training should be viewed as another tool in your toolbox of skills and resources, not as the cure-all for employee problems. Many times, employees' problems are a direct result of their supervisors' leadership or management style. Before sending an employee off to training for a "quick fix," thoroughly assess the situation.

Do any of these excuses sound familiar? If you said yes, you're not alone. The next time you hear your peers using statements like these— COACH them!

Review & Practice

Think about your relationship with your employees. Examine the excuses below and see if you can invalidate them in your own work environment:

1. "It takes too long."
Why this excuse is not valid:

_____

_____

2. "If employees need help, they'll ask."
Why this excuse is not valid:

_____

_____

3. "I don't know how."
Why this excuse is not valid:

_____

_____

4. "Employees might think I don't trust them."
Why this excuse is not valid:

_____

_____

1

5. "I've got other more important things to do."
Why this excuse is not valid:

_____

_____

6. "It's the trainer's job to teach skills."
Why this excuse is not valid:

_____

_____

Action Plan for Coaching

To be sure you have not been neglecting your coaching responsibilities, think about specific employees you feel you should be coaching more. List their names and reasons for coaching them for future reference. As you work through this book, you will learn concrete strategies for coaching these and future employees.

Employee	Reason for Coaching
_____	_____
_____	_____
_____	_____
_____	_____
_____	_____
_____	_____
_____	_____
_____	_____
_____	_____
_____	_____
_____	_____
_____	_____
_____	_____
_____	_____
_____	_____
_____	_____

Expanding What You Have Learned

Take a few minutes to reinforce some of the concepts and ideas we have covered by answering the following questions. If you do not currently supervise others, project how you think you would handle the situations:

1. Coaching is a developmental process. To be effective, there must be ongoing one-on-one communication. What are you currently doing to guide your employees?

   _____

   _____

2. Organizational structures are changing rapidly. These changes have necessitated shifts in the way employees are managed. Think about changes in supervisory roles that you have seen or experienced in your organization. What other changes do you think will occur in those roles by the next decade? How will you handle them?

   _____

   _____

3. Numerous benefits are gained by coaching. What is the best way to communicate these benefits to your employees and gain their support of your coaching efforts?

   _____

   _____

1

4. It is often easy to find excuses for not coaching employees. Picture your workplace during the past four weeks. Have you or has anyone else used any excuses not to coach? What are three specific strategies you can implement to make sure that these excuses are not repeated?

_____

_____

5. Opportunities to coach arise daily if you are attuned to them. Think about your current work environment. List at least four situations that will allow you to coach your employees.

_____

_____

Chapter 1 Checkpoints

✓ Maintain regular interpersonal communication with your employees.

✓ Be constantly alert to changing situations that could signal a need to coach employees.

✓ Don't lose sight of the benefits to be gained from coaching. By using coaching, you set up a potential win-win environment for yourself and for your employees.

✓ Avoid the temptation to delay or ignore the need for coaching.

2 Opportunities for Coaching

This chapter will help you to:

- Realize the cost of failing to coach effectively.
- Recognize opportunities for coaching employees.
- Develop a strategy for orienting new employees.
- Explain the importance of developing current employees' performance.

Things have been changing rapidly at ComputerLand, Ltd. Sam McKinney has been a supervisor for five years and is amazed at the ongoing additions to product lines, services, and employees. The third takeover of a competing company in the past two years was completed last week.

Sam has always been proud of his accomplishments. And even though his store has been named "Store of the Quarter" every quarter for the past year, he is becoming concerned over high turnover in his sales staff. Although higher-than-usual movement of personnel is common for sales professionals, lately someone always seems to be coming or going.

With his responsibilities for monitoring sales and training new salespeople, Sam barely has time for anything else. He knows he should spend more time with all his employees, but he never seems to be able to get to them.

Sam's boss, Jill Columbo, visited him this week. She wanted to know what was causing the high employee turnover and subsequent lower morale. She has heard rumors that employees feel they are not getting management support or adequate training, yet are expected to "be the best." ■

Questions to Consider

1. What can Sam tell Jill?

_____

_____

_____

2. Is there anything that Sam can do to remedy the situation?

_____

_____

_____

3. Is there anything Jill can do to help? If so, what?

_____

_____

_____

THE COST OF FAILING TO COACH

In Chapter 1 you explored some of the benefits derived from coaching. In addition, coaching cuts costs. With the costs of recruitment, hiring, and employee benefits growing higher each day, supervisors must protect the investments of their organization. Each time an employee leaves, replacement costs escalate. The following example illustrates what a lost employee costs an organization. Use the table to compute the costs your organization incurs when replacing an employee. Compute local costs for your area and include any special expenditures that you encounter when hiring for a specific position.

Position: Secretary with Basic Software Experience

To be hired from outside the organization within three weeks.

Expenditure	Cost
Advertising	$ 560.00
Interviewing (human resources personnel and managers' time, plus time for background checks, testing, etc.)	375.00
Support staff time	45.00
Fees for background and credit checks/testing	125.00
Orientation (trainers'/employees' salaries, materials, facilities, and equipment)	325.00
On-the-job training	500.00
Total	$1930.00

RECOGNIZING OPPORTUNITIES FOR COACHING

By now you probably have begun to recognize that there are numerous advantages to communicating regularly with employees. At least one advantage is the ability to be absent from the workplace while still having your objectives met. This becomes possible when you have developed your employees to perform on their own. To ensure the likelihood of this occurring, you must be continually on the lookout for opportunities to guide, train, and cultivate your team members. It should not be hard to find such opportunities since they occur on a daily basis in any work environment.

Whether being used to help orient a new employee or to assist tenured employees learn new skills or build on current ones, coaching is an effective management tool. In fact, frequent use of coaching can eliminate the need for much formal employee retraining or counseling later on. It is far more productive and easier to deal with a deficiency while it is still small than having to address it as a full-blown problem.

A good rule of thumb is to consider coaching whenever **any** type of **change** occurs. Look at the following list of typical instances that require coaching. Can you think of others?

- A new employee joins your team.
- A tenured employee is being considered for a new position.
- A new policy or procedure is being implemented.
- Technology is changed or added to the workplace.
- Departmental/corporate strategic goals/objectives are changed.
- A new supervisor is added to the work unit.
- Training has been conducted and you want to continue raising job skills through follow-up.
- New tasks are assigned.
- You have an average or below-average performer.
- You are building teams.
- A merger, downsizing, expansion, or relocation is occurring within the organization.
- A special project is upcoming.
- Good performance needs to be reinforced.

Before going further, select all the instances from the above list that are, or will be, occurring in your workplace. On separate sheets of paper, list each of these situations, along with at least three coaching strategies that you could use to address them. By thinking about these now, you are developing strategies for potential future situations.

ORIENTING NEW EMPLOYEES

Think back to the first week you were on your current or previous job.

1. What was done by the supervisor to make you feel welcome?
2. How long did it take for your formal orientation?
3. How much time did your new supervisor actually spend with you?
4. Was a peer coach assigned to you? What was his or her role? How well did he or she fulfill that role?
5. If you did have a peer coach, how could he or she have been more effective?
6. What type of information did you receive about the company, department, job, benefits, and so forth?
7. What information or materials would have made your transition into the new environment more effective?

With this image fresh in your mind, think about how you handle employee orientations. Your coaching relationships begin when new employees join your team. From the first day you must assume certain coaching-related responsibilities. Failure to do so often results in frustration and inability for you or the employee to succeed. Remember that while you are sizing up your new employees, they are sizing you up. And with the high costs of employee replacement illustrated earlier, it is foolhardy to act in an unconcerned manner.

THE ORIENTATION PROCESS

Your orientation process should make new employees feel welcome and confident about you and the organization. The primary purpose of the orientation is to provide a period of transition and to transform an outsider into a loyal, productive employee. To meet these objectives, you must be cautious not to project a disorganized image when introducing the new employee into the workplace. Remember, first impressions are lasting. A seemingly disjointed orientation can send a negative message to your new employee.

While much will be learned from fellow workers, the initial tasks of greeting and orienting new employees are too important for you to

delegate. You should personally ensure that a solid initial foundation is set when an employee joins your team.

Employees are most in need of your support and encouragement during the orientation period. During this time, they form attitudes about you and the organization, so it becomes important for you to acclimate and orient new members of your staff properly. Use the following checklist to be sure that you have not forgotten to cover vital information.

▮ Departmental Orientation Checklist

- ☐ Welcome the new employee.
- ☐ Discuss departmental goals and objectives.
- ☐ Explain operational procedures and activities.
- ☐ Introduce products, services, and customer base.
- ☐ Define the relationship of jobs within the department (structure).
- ☐ Delineate the relationship of the employee's job with other departments.
- ☐ Outline job duties, responsibilities, and standards.
- ☐ Point out common problem areas to avoid.
- ☐ Talk over performance evaluation procedures.
- ☐ Detail supervisors' expectations.
- ☐ Present the employee's work schedule.
- ☐ Summarize required paperwork and reports.
- ☐ Go over procedure for requisition of supplies and services.
- ☐ Define corporate policies and procedures that affect the department.
- ☐ Go over emergency procedures and safety precautions.
- ☐ Set forth departmental norms (cleanliness, attendance, smoking, security, breaks, lunch, personal calls).
- ☐ Conduct a tour of the department and make introductions to co-workers and key customers.
- ☐ Assign a "buddy" to facilitate orientation.
- ☐ Schedule a follow-up meeting with the employee within one week to answer questions and get feedback.

Because the orientation process is usually divided into distinct components, careful coordination must be made with the human resources department to ensure complete coverage of information.

Phases of an Orientation

Phase 1: General Company Orientation.   This phase normally is conducted by the human resources department and actually begins before the employee is hired. During the interview process applicants are given an overview of the company and its products and services. After being hired, employees generally are given a more in-depth orientation, including information about benefits, compensation, policies, and procedures. Employees may be provided with an orientation kit that contains reference information about the organization.

Phase 2: Supervisor Orientation.   This phase is your responsibility. The new team member is introduced into the work-unit culture, receives an explanation about operational procedures, and gets specific job-related guidance. Normally you and/or a competent employee peer coach conduct this orientation.

GETTING HELP WITH ORIENTATION

As mentioned earlier, many supervisors use the peer-coaching or "buddy" system. This practice is widespread and works well if you carefully select and train the "buddies" before having them interact officially with new employees. The selectee(s) should understand the importance of their assignment and responsibilities. The following checklist will help you select future peer coaches:

2

Buddy Selection Checklist

The buddy:

- ☐ Has a positive attitude about his or her supervisor, the job, and the organization.
- ☐ Wants to be a peer coach.
- ☐ Accepts responsibility.
- ☐ Is an excellent listener and communicator.
- ☐ Has a solid knowledge of policies, procedures, and departmental/organizational goals.
- ☐ Is technically qualified.
- ☐ Is personable.
- ☐ Is patient.
- ☐ Is fair, honest, and dependable.
- ☐ Is a good role model.
- ☐ Demonstrates initiative.
- ☐ Is creative and visionary.
- ☐ Understands how adults learn.
- ☐ Is an analytical thinker.
- ☐ Is cost conscious.
- ☐ Is accurate.
- ☐ Is a top performer.

Other characteristics:

Many supervisors make the mistake of assigning any available employee to "show the new person around." Often, the departing employee for whose position the new person has been hired is used as a coach. There is a potential for disaster here since the departing employee may have a bad attitude about you or the department. Also, the departing employee has little to lose by sharing negative wisdom or shortcuts (usually unauthorized) to established procedures. In effect, you could be setting a new employee up for failure from the start. If employees learn an unauthorized technique or information from their buddy, their own performance evaluation could suffer later. As a result, they could develop their own negative attitude or performance pattern.

That is the downside. From a positive perspective, a carefully screened and qualified buddy can provide a positive role model for the new employee. Additionally, many long hours of supervisor coaching and counseling can be eliminated if the new employee gets a solid beginning.

A word of caution when orienting a new employee, especially an interdepartmental transfer or one with job-related experience: ASSUME NOTHING! Even if an employee has worked in another job or department in the organization or has held a similar job elsewhere, he or she has not done the present job with you. Policies, procedures, and leadership styles often vary greatly between organizations and individuals. Standards used by another department, individual, or similar organization may not meet your criteria. Old techniques must often be unlearned when a new employee joins your team.

DEVELOPING CURRENT EMPLOYEES

Supervisors are often blocked from taking vacations, special assignments, and even promotions because there is no one qualified within the organization to step into their position. To prevent this from happening to you, examine your role(s) and relationship with your tenured employees.

Once a new employee is adequately settled into the organization, the supervisor-employee relationship evolves, and you should consider refocusing your efforts. Your new objective should be to help employees perform at higher levels and seek further growth. By encouraging them to strive for more responsibility, you are helping prepare them for future assignments and positions. Additionally, you are preparing them potentially to replace you on a temporary or permanent basis.

To increase your chances for success, you must not lose sight of the importance of having written attainable goals for each employee. Many supervisors forget that coaching is a joint venture and leave the employee out of the planning and goal-setting phase. Develop goals *with* employees; do not assign goals *to* your employees. It is difficult for employees to do a good job if their hearts are not in it.

Assuming that employees do buy in to jointly established goals, they can still run into frustration because they don't get the appropriate guidance and coaching as they proceed. In many instances, a few well-chosen words of praise on a regular basis from you is all that is needed. Even if the job is only partially correct, you should recognize that success and then coach the employee to redirect his or her behavior in order to correct any deficiency. Some positive reinforcement is better than none. The obvious result of such action is a more satisfied employee and a supervisor who doesn't have to work so hard on counseling poor performers. As you work with your employees to plan and improve their performance, you will find their confidence and trust levels rise.

Expanding What You Have Learned

1. Opportunities to coach employees continually arise. What are some situations in your organization that will allow you to apply some of the information covered in this chapter?

   _____

   _____

2. The costs of recruiting and retaining a new employee continue to go up. What are some things you can do to help new employees while holding costs down in your organization and positioning yourself as an efficient supervisor in the eyes of your boss?

   _____

   _____

3. Too often we neglect new employees even though we mean to eventually get around to talking with them. List several ways you will prevent this from occurring with your new employees.

   _____

   _____

4. As a supervisor, you assume many roles in dealing with employees. Which roles do you feel are most important and how do you address them in the workplace?

_____

_____

2

Chapter 2 Checkpoints

✓ Coaching is a cost-effective means of developing and keeping good employees.

✓ Any time change occurs, consider coaching your employees.

✓ Your coaching relationship begins with the orientation of new employees. Don't miss this important opportunity to develop rapport.

✓ When choosing peer coaches, select wisely.

✓ One way of assuring your own professional mobility is to prepare your employees to take on your job responsibilities.

3 A Model for Effective Coaching

This chapter will help you to:

- Develop a systematic approach to coaching, using a formal eight-phase model.
- Set effective goals and objectives with your employees.
- Identify resources for employee development.
- Construct with your employees an action plan for employee development.

Armando Santiago is a supervisor in the reproduction department of a large nonprofit organization. He is very conscientious and feels that he does a good job supervising his employees. As evidence of this, he points out that he tries to stop by each employee's work station at least once or twice a week to say hello.

Armando has recently been concerned about the performance of an experienced press operator, Lawrence Miller. Since installation of new equipment several months ago, the quality and quantity of Lawrence's work have fallen. Armando has stopped by Lawrence's work station several times recently to ask, "How's it going?" Lawrence traditionally replies, "Fine." Armando hoped that by giving Lawrence an opportunity to explain the change in his work output, things could be resolved. Although he hates to do it, Armando is frustrated and plans to officially counsel Lawrence for poor performance. ∎

Questions to Consider

1. What are the issues in this scenario?

_____

_____

_____

2. Do you feel that Armando is doing a good job of coaching?

_____

_____

_____

3. If you were Armando's manager, what action might you take? Why?

_____

_____

_____

4. What can Armando do to help Lawrence?

_____

_____

_____

THE COACHING PROCESS MODEL (CPM)

As with any other successful initiative, supervisors need to use a systematic process when coaching. This is necessary to accurately assess employees' performance and develop strategies for continued improvement. The coaching process model (CPM) is designed to provide you and your employees a vehicle for success.

By following each phase of the CPM, you and your employees progress toward increased effectiveness and efficiency. Notice that one common element interwoven throughout all eight phases of the model is feedback. Feedback is a crucial aspect in any supervisor-employee interaction and should **never** be omitted.

Phase 1: Establish Goals.   Work with the employee to establish reasonable, attainable performance goals. Consider the person's job description, the needs of the organization, established job standards, resources, time, and any other appropriate variable when establishing the goals.

A simple technique for developing a performance goal is to ensure that it is:

- Realistic and attainable in terms of the employee's ability, skills, available time, and desires.
- Measurable by factors such as time, money, quantity, or quality.

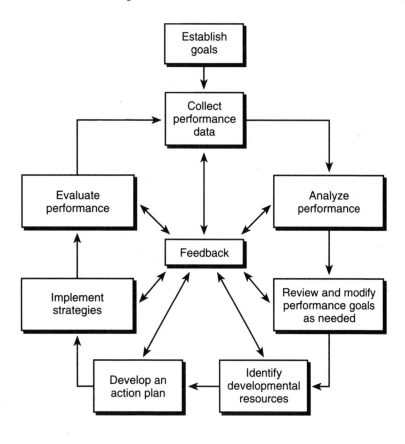

- Specific in defining exactly what performance is expected.
- Focused with a specific target date for completion.

Phase 2: Collect Performance Data. You have an ongoing obligation to study your employees' behavior in order to determine on-the-job performance. Your purpose is to gather all available information for use in phase 3 of the process. Gathering large amounts of data helps ensure a more thorough analysis of performance. Here are some of the methods for gathering data:

- Customer surveys.
- Personal observation.
- Interviews (peers/employee/other supervisors).
- Performance appraisals.
- Reports.
- Self-assessment questionnaires.

Setting Realistic Performance Goals

Too often, supervisors and employees agree to performance goals that are unreasonable and unattainable. This is a prescription for failure. When employees fail to reach established goals, they often become discouraged, demoralized, and unproductive.

Instead of putting the bar too high and expecting employees to jump over it, look at the average performance of other similarly qualified employees who are performing similar tasks. Then thoroughly scrutinize all performance data outlined in phase 2 of the CPM and make an educated determination on logical courses of action.

Examine performance closely

Phase 3: Analyze Performance.   Once you have successfully collected information about an employee's performance, you can move on to the analysis phase. Your purpose is to identify those areas where the employee is meeting or exceeding expectations and those areas where he or she is deficient. Deficiencies are called *performance gaps*. Any developmental need identified as a deficiency will be addressed in phase 4, when performance goals are reviewed and modified with the employee in order to improve behavior.

It is an important part of your analysis to consider all factors that may be affecting the employee's performance, either positively or negatively. Some potential influences include the following:

- Supervisory coaching (or lack of it).
- Employee knowledge or skills.
- Employee disabilities.
- Changes in the workplace/organization (structure, policies, procedures, personnel, technology).
- Customers.
- Special projects or assignments.

3

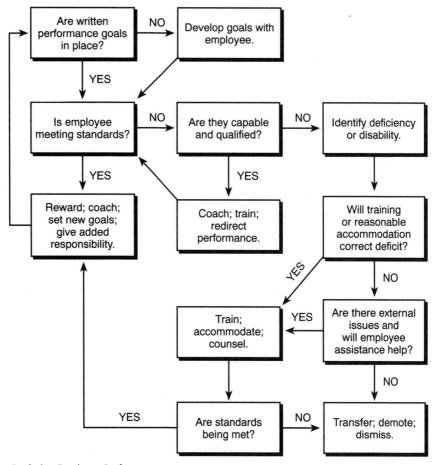

Analyzing Employee Performance

Phase 4: Review and Modify Performance Goals as Needed. Based on identified deficits found between actual and desired performance, your next step is to schedule a meeting to coach your employee and redefine

3

goals as necessary. During this meeting, provide specific feedback on your observations. Solicit employee feedback, then jointly determine reasonable, attainable goals for future on-the-job efforts.

Phase 5: Identify Developmental Resources.   Many resources and techniques are available for teaching the necessary knowledge and skills your employees need. Depending on time, funding, employee deficiency, and general organizational atmosphere, determine which techniques are the most viable. Implement appropriate training techniques using behavioral objectives as a measure of success. The table below identifies some potential developmental options.

Resources for Employee Development

On the Job	Off the Job
■ One-on-one supervisor coaching.	■ College courses.
■ Job rotation.	■ Professional seminars.
■ Job enrichment.	■ Professional organizations.
■ Role-plays.	■ Networking.
■ Case studies.	■ Professional certificate programs.
■ Computer-assisted instruction (CAI).	■ Field trips.
■ Programmed instruction (textbook courses).	■ Correspondence courses.
■ Lectures.	■ Research/writing assignments.
■ Organization-sponsored training.	
■ In-basket exercises.	
■ Special projects/assignments.	
■ Reference material review.	
■ Mentoring.	

Phase 6: Develop an Action Plan.   With employee goals, resources, and identified employee needs in mind, work with the employee to develop an action plan that is both effective and efficient. The plan should not be complicated, and there **must** be commitment on both sides for it to work. The chart below illustrates a potential action plan format:

Action Plan for Employee Development

Identify Current Strengths/Competence Levels   What is going well? How well are tasks being performed? These questions are answered in phase 3 of the coaching process model.

_____

_____

_____

Identify Need(s)   List specific knowledge, skills, or attitudes to be addressed with employee development activities.

_____

_____

_____

Establish Performance Goals   Use current goals as a basis, if they exist. Develop goals that address identified needs.

_____

_____

_____

Select Development Activities   List specific resources, strategies, and initiatives that will be used to develop the employee. Specify dates for future meetings to reassess progress.

_____

_____

_____

Select Target Date(s) for Completion   List the due date(s) for completion of each task.

_____

_____

_____

Phase 7: Implement Strategies.   Once an action plan is in place, ensure that the employee has the necessary tools, information, and support needed to succeed. As part of the implementation, take care to establish the proper setting for success:

- *Describe the specific skill desired of the employee.* By letting the person know what is expected of him or her in advance, in a non-threatening manner, you give him or her the opportunity to visualize the goal before being confronted with the task.

- *Demonstrate the skill.* Model the exact behavior that the employee is to copy. If necessary, repeat the demonstration several times until the person is comfortable with what is expected.

- *Solicit feedback.* Make sure that the employee has grasped the task instructions and process.

- *Have the employee perform the task.* In your presence, have the person repeat what you have demonstrated.

- *Provide feedback on performance.* Take care to use positive feedback for a job well done and constructive criticism for incorrectly performed tasks. In a learning environment, it is important to praise any portion of the task that is performed correctly and to redirect instructions for those portions not completely right. It is better to give partial praise than none at all.

- *Modify the training activity if necessary.* Chances are the employee won't get everything right the first time. Be patient and willing to redemonstrate or change your approach if it will help comprehension. The final reward for the extra effort is a more productive employee who ultimately will make your job easier.

Phase 8: Evaluate Performance.   By using measurable standards, you can assess your employee's success or failure. If at any point during the developmental activity, it becomes obvious that the employee may not succeed in reaching the goals, you and the employee should discuss the reason before continuing. Once the task is completed, determine the result, then give specific and immediate feedback. If the employee has not attained the agreed-upon performance levels, repeat as many steps in the CPM as required to boost outcome.

Expanding What You Have Learned

Now that you have read the formal coaching process model, take a few minutes to list the steps you currently take to determine employee performance levels. Also think about how you go about addressing any deficiencies you discover.

1. How do you currently determine an employee's performance level?

_____

_____

2. Once you have identified the employee's performance level, how do you decide how well employees are performing?

_____

_____

3. By comparing past and current performance to future projected changes, you can pinpoint developmental needs. What are some of the changes in your workplace that could influence employee performance?

_____

_____

4. To address performance needs, employees need specific goals. How do you currently set employee goals?

_____

_____

5. We often overlook important resources that can help improve employee performance. What resources do you use to assist your employees?

_____

_____

6. Employees often need a nudge or show of support from their supervisor before working actively toward performance improvement. What do you currently do to encourage development?

_____

_____

Compare your responses to the CPM. Make any modifications necessary to improve your current methods.

Chapter 3 Checkpoints

✓ Before beginning any coaching activity, always gather valid performance data.

✓ Use information about employees' performance to analyze how well they are meeting established standards.

✓ Goal setting is done **with** and not **to** employees in order to gain commitment.

✓ Consider a variety of resources and techniques for sharing knowledge or teaching skills.

✓ Set an action plan that will assist employees in becoming proficient at assigned tasks.

✓ Take the time to instruct and coach employees when they are performing new tasks.

✓ At designated deadline dates, evaluate employees' progress using measurable criteria.

4 | Building Interpersonal Relationships

This chapter will help you to:

- Explain how coaching can aid in building better relationships.
- Use your knowledge of communication to improve interpersonal relationships in the workplace.
- Learn to avoid the "Nine Deadly Sins" that affect relationships.
- Build stronger relationships with your peers and with your boss.

Tina Anderson has been supervisor of nursing at a large metropolitan hospital for the past two years. Before her promotion, she had over seven years' experience as a clinical nurse with several different medical facilities. Tina tries hard to be a good "people person" and considers herself successful in that area, although she doesn't have many close relationships at the hospital. She attributes her lack of closeness with peers and employees to be a byproduct of working a rotating shift schedule.

Carla Wyatt, the director of nursing and Tina's boss, recently had a performance meeting with Tina to discuss a pattern that seems to be forming. In the meeting, Carla shared the results of a recent employee exit-interview summary that showed comments from departing employees. Over the past two years there have been numerous remarks concerning Tina's communication style and personality, such as, "Tina is very aloof," "Tina never takes time to share information with me," and, "It feels like Tina doesn't really care about people, just getting the job done." In addition to these comments, Carla shared that other supervisors had labeled Tina "a loner."

When she heard these comments, Tina was shocked. She couldn't imagine why people would say or think such things about her. She stated, "I go out of my way to say good morning, and I assign people to organize a luncheon whenever someone has a birthday." ■

Questions to Consider

1. What seem to be the issues in this scenario?

_____

_____

_____

2. What do you think Tina could do differently?

_____

_____

_____

3. What do you think Tina is doing well?

_____

_____

_____

4. If you were Carla, what would you do or say?

_____

_____

_____

COACHING FOR BETTER RELATIONSHIPS

Better interpersonal relationships are a natural outcome of effective coaching. Most people will appreciate your interest and concern for them. Some general tips for effective coaching follow:

- Establish solid two-way communication.
- Develop trust with employees.
- Acknowledge accomplishments and sacrifices.
- Openly solicit ideas, suggestions, and criticisms.
- Listen to what others have to say.

- Provide an open-door policy for performance problems.
- Determine guidelines to follow in completing assignments.
- Set realistic goals when assigning tasks.
- Check for employee understanding of instructions.
- Give honest and fair feedback on an ongoing basis.
- Allow room for personal and professional growth.
- Involve others in your decision making.
- Teach simple, basic ideas, concepts, or techniques first; then follow up with more advanced strategies.
- Whenever employees appear to be in a slump, coach them.
- Use successful employees as mentors or peer coaches.
- Act as a resource to employees, peers, and your boss.

THE IMPORTANCE OF SOLID COMMUNICATION

As you can see, most of the above tips deal with communication skills. Without the ability to receive information accurately through focused listening and to send messages in an easily understood manner, your chances of successful coaching are virtually eliminated. For effective one-on-one communication, several key elements must be present. Each is highlighted in the two-way communication model shown below:

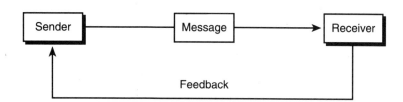

If any of the elements in the model are missing, interpersonal communication cannot take place and relationships will break down. In coaching, whether you are the sender or the receiver of a message, you play a crucial part in the success or failure of an interaction. Failure to send a message in a clear, concise manner or to listen effectively and provide feedback ends the conversation or exchange of information. Keep in mind that perceptions people have about you or your actions dictate how they perceive your intent—perceptions are reality. Your success depends on others.

Are You a Good Communicator?

Think about how you currently communicate, and circle T for true or F for false for each of the following statements:

T   F   **1.** I always stop what I am doing when someone talks to me.

T   F   **2.** I strive to listen to the words and emotions of the sender in all interactions.

T   F   **3.** I am conscious of the nonverbal messages I send through various vocal qualities and my body language.

T   F   **4.** I think consciously about the best time and place to deliver my message before I send it.

T   F   **5.** I consider alternative methods of message delivery and choose the one that will have the greatest effect and benefit.

T   F   **6.** I always follow through on promises in order to foster trust.

T   F   **7.** I am conscious of the feelings of others.

T   F   **8.** I openly solicit and act on advice from others.

T   F   **9.** I solicit and give honest feedback when communicating with others.

T   F   **10.** I encourage others to be all they can be and I assist in their development.

If you answered "true" to all of the statements, you are probably on your way to building powerful relationships. If you answered "false" to any of the statements, you need to work on improving your communication skills.

DEVELOPING SOUND RELATIONSHIPS

Your relationships with others depend primarily on the way you and they view, perceive, and react to each other. Here are some factors that affect all relationships:

- *Effective one-on-one communication (verbal, nonverbal, and vocal qualities).* This is the thread that holds the relationship together.

- *Psychological profile of each party involved.* Beliefs, values, past experiences, education, personal aspirations, emotions, and biases all play a role in building or destroying relationships.

- *Role(s) assumed by or assigned to each participant.* Growth of relationships depends on the status or perceived status and behavior of each person involved.

- *Perceived value of the relationship.* If you and your employee believe there is mutual benefit to be gained by working together, you are likely to try harder during interactions.

4

Nine Deadly Sins That Affect Relationships

1. *Failing to Communicate Effectively.* Unless regular communication occurs, relationships often falter.

2. *Playing Games.* There must be mutual trust and respect for a relationship to develop and survive. If either party damages either of these, there surely will be negative consequences and retribution.

3. *Playing Favorites.* As a supervisor, you must be constantly alert to unfair or perceived unfair behavior. You cannot afford to sacrifice one employee relationship for another. You need all of your employees to support you, and vice versa.

4. *Getting Involved with Employees' Personal Problems.* Your job is to help employees perform successfully. You should not get caught up in the personal problems of one or two employees. Others depend on you sharing your time with them. When personal problems affect performance, refer the employee to the human resources department for assistance.

5. *Becoming Personally Involved with Employees.* Getting involved in a personal or intimate relationship is a sure way to create problems with the employees you become involved with and with their peers.

6. *Ignoring Performance Gaps.* If it becomes evident that an employee is not meeting established standards or agreed upon goals, take immediate action. The problem will not go away, but could grow.

7. *Treating Employees Unfairly.* Most employees will go along with your decisions if they believe you are acting fairly. Taking time to explain why you did or did not take an action often ensures acceptance.

8. *Failing to Build a Sound Foundation.* As you saw in Chapter 2, the ideal time to begin your relationship with an employee is during orientation.

9. *Displaying a Lackadaisical Attitude.* If employees perceive that they are not important or that you have priorities above them and their needs, you may lose their trust and loyalty.

Keep in mind that all of the issues and techniques for building effective relationships with employees also apply to relationships with peers and with your boss.

HELPING YOUR PEERS

How often have you observed a colleague unknowingly making a mistake? Did you say anything and give constructive criticism, or did you do nothing? If you did nothing, ask yourself why. Were you:

- Happy they were having problems because it made you look better?
- Too embarrassed to say anything?
- Afraid you would hurt their feelings?
- Too busy to help?
- Indifferent?
- Unsure how to broach the subject with them?
- Concerned they would get upset?
- Worried that you did not have any valuable solutions to offer?
- Just too lazy to do it?!

Whatever the reason, you did your co-worker, yourself, and the organization an injustice. Other than the individual's boss, few people are better prepared to assist and give meaningful feedback than a trained fellow supervisor. You are paid for, and experienced in, providing performance feedback and support. Whether with an employee or with a peer, take the time to do your part. If done tactfully, your efforts likely will be appreciated.

■ Your Experience

To see the value of peer coaching, think about a time when you made a bad judgment call, dealt with a new assignment, or had to take action in an unfamiliar situation. Write an overview of what happened. Then answer the following questions concerning the event:

1. How did you handle the situation?

_____

_____

2. In retrospect, what could you have done differently or better?

_____

_____

4

3. Did anyone give you guidance? If so, who?

_____

_____

4. Were there any peers available who were equally or more experienced in handling similar situations?

_____

_____

5. If you answered yes to number 4, did you solicit or receive their help? Explain the results of their involvement.

_____

_____

6. If the answer to number 4 was no, could their assistance have made you more successful or changed the outcome of the situation? How?

_____

_____

Too often, we are reluctant either to solicit or to accept help from peers. When one of these instances occurs, everyone loses. If you fail to ask, you miss out on the benefit of another person's ideas or knowledge and an opportunity to strengthen a peer relationship. If your peers fail to offer, they miss an opportunity to strengthen a peer relationship, to learn from the situation, to share their knowledge, and to help you in achieving an organizational goal.

As part of management, you should strive to help all employees, not just direct reports. One of your roles is to use your knowledge, skills, and expertise as a supervisor to better position the organization in a competitive environment. Failing to assist peers and fulfill this organizational role ultimately positions you as a self-serving individual rather than as a valu-able team player. In the long run, being seen as self-serving will only increase your chances of failing.

ADVISING THE BOSS

Another of your key roles is to advise your boss. Because of your knowl-edge, skill, and frontline exposure to employees, you are one of the most qualified members of your organization to consult with the boss on employee-related issues. Any boss worth his or her salary knows this and regularly taps into this supervisory information bank. For that reason, you must constantly be alert to changes in the workplace and you should stay current on the latest strategies, systems, trends, and techniques for improved employee performance in your industry.

Knowledge is power. How powerful are you? What are some potential situations in which the boss might ask for your assistance? Are you knowl-edgeable enought to give sound advice in each of these situations? If you answered no, you may want to consider some self-development activities to gain necessary knowledge or skills to prepare for future opportunities.

Here are some questions you can ask to strengthen relationships.

Relationship-Building Questions

- How can I communicate with you more effectively?
- What can I do to help you become more successful in your job?
- What can I do to help you develop professionally?
- How can I support your efforts in the workplace?
- Is there anything I can do to make your job more fun?
- What equipment, materials, or knowledge can I provide that will increase your productivity/service levels?
- What can I do to make/keep our relationship positive?

■ Expanding What You Have Learned

1. What is your normal means of communicating with others? Is it the most effective way to build stronger relationships?

_____

_____

2. Are you guilty of any of the nine deadly sins that affect relationships? If so, how can you eliminate them?

_____

_____

3. Do you consciously consider factors that affect relationships in order to avoid possible failure of a relationship?

_____

_____

4. In addition to your employees, your peers and your boss depend on you for developmental support. What are you currently doing to fulfill that support role? What can you do differently?

_____

_____

4

Chapter 4 Checkpoints

✓ Sound communication takes two committed parties—a sender and a receiver.

✓ Committing one or more of the nine deadly sins that affect relationships can contribute to your failure as a coach.

✓ Be aware of the factors that affect relationships and use them to your advantage.

✓ Look for opportunities to assist your employees, your peers, and your boss.

✓ Peers can benefit significantly from your objective observations and feedback.

✓ Do not hesitate to share knowledge and information with your boss. He or she will remember you for the effort.

5 | Effective Feedback Strategies

This chapter will help you to:

- Recognize various types of feedback.
- Identify strategies for giving and receiving feedback.
- Give praise effectively.
- Give criticism constructively.
- Develop an environment that encourages the use of feedback.

Harold Labronski was having a terrible day at the warehouse. As the supervisor of a 20-person work team, he felt overwhelmed. Deadlines and quotas were missed due to increased shipping orders, a holiday last week caused delivery backups, and four people were out sick this week. On top of all this, someone had run into his parked car last night.

Tom Schneider, who has been with the company for three years and is a dependable worker, arrived 30 minutes late for work today—the second time this month he has had trouble with his car. This is only his third tardiness since joining the company. He has decided it is time to trade the car in rather than face further problems.

As soon as Harold spotted Tom, he yelled across the warehouse, "Schneider! In my office, NOW!" Tom was a bit confused by Harold's tone, but dutifully proceeded to the office. Upon arrival, Tom attempted to greet Harold and explain his tardiness but was cut off by a screaming tirade from Harold. "This has got to stop. You're *always* coming in late. How are we supposed to get work done when you're not here?" ■

Questions to Consider

1. What are some issues in this scenario?

_____

_____

_____

2. How do you think Harold handled the situation with Tom?

_____

_____

_____

3. What could have been done differently by Harold? By Tom?

_____

_____

_____

Think about times when you have been involved in situations like the one just described. Focus on developing a plan for handling such situations in the future as you go through this chapter.

WHAT IS FEEDBACK?

As you saw earlier, feedback is an integral component of both the coaching process model and the two-way communication model. This is because feedback is the only indication that the message you intend to send is received correctly. Feedback is also an effective tool for developing and reinforcing the relationships discussed in Chapter 4. Occasionally, confusion may result when you and your employee interact. Lack of appropriate feedback is often the culprit. There are potentially four messages in any two-way conversation:

1. The message you intended to send.
2. The message received by your employee.
3. The feedback message your employee intended to send back to you.
4. The message you received.

Numerous factors affect feedback and cause message breakdown. When coaching or communicating with others, thinking about the following causes of miscommunication may help overcome problems:

- Poor listening habits.
- Differing backgrounds (education, socioeconomic, values, beliefs, and experiences).
- Gender differences.
- Improper selection of time and location for message delivery.
- Improper selection of method for delivering the message.
- Stress and preconceived ideas (such as in Harold's case earlier).
- Distractions.
- Biases/prejudices.

HOW TO GIVE FEEDBACK

It is impossible for you to "not communicate." Your words and actions are constantly being received and interpreted in different ways by others. Here are a few of the channels through which you send messages:

- **Written Correspondence.** Your style of writing, quantity of output, and the way you express yourself (language, grammar, semantics) communicate things about yourself.
- **Verbal Communication.** You send messages through the words you choose (semantics) and the quality of your voice (tone, rate, volume, pitch, articulation).
- **Nonverbal Communication.** Your gestures, body positioning, proximity to the employee, eye contact, and physical contact send powerful messages.
- **Actions/Inactions.** By either taking or failing to take action, especially if you promised to do something, you send a message of either importance or irrelevance.
- **Trappings.** Your clothing, car, office (size, furnishings, organization), jewelry, and other personal items send messages.

APPROACHES TO FEEDBACK

To increase your effectiveness, try using the following strategies when giving performance feedback to others:

- *Focus on the person's behavior, not the person.* Your purpose is to improve behavior, not to shame or distance the person from you.

You should address the behavior observed and work toward helping improve it, if necessary. *Example of shaming:* "You are such a jerk!" Instead, try, "Sometimes I don't know why you do certain things. Can you help me understand?"

- *Avoid globalizing the behavior.* Globalization creates barriers to effectiveness, causes defensiveness, and often provokes retaliation. It is unlikely that the employee *always* or *never* does something (as in Harold's case earlier). *Examples of globalization:* "You always do . . ." "You never do . . ." Instead, try, "Occasionally, when you do . . . I get frustrated because . . ."

- *Use* I *instead of* you *language.* It is difficult for someone to dispute or argue with the way you personally feel or with observable facts. *You* terminology can sound very threatening and accusatory, creating defensiveness, anger, or feelings of retaliation. *Examples of I language:* "*I* feel that this was caused by . . . ," "*I* was disappointed that you . . ."

USING FEEDBACK EFFECTIVELY

Feedback is a powerful tool that can enhance or destroy relationships with others. To make sure that the outcomes of your communication are effective, think before you speak. Consider these questions:

- *Is this the right time to give this feedback?* When someone is busy, upset, frustrated, or generally not ready to receive your message, you are wasting your time and possibly could defeat your own intent by giving feedback.

- *Is this the right place?* Depending on the type of feedback, you may be better off moving to another location or postponing the feedback. This is especially true when giving criticism. Never give it in front of other people. A rule of thumb: praise in public, criticize in private.

- *Is this the appropriate person to whom I should give this feedback?* When angry or frustrated, we sometimes need to unload or get something off our chest, so we dump on the first person we see. Not only is this ineffective and unnecessary, it is unfair. Count to ten, think, then address the issue with the proper person.

- *What is the best way to communicate my message?* Face-to-face is the preferred method for message delivery because it allows verbal and nonverbal feedback. Other options include communicating over the telephone, via fax, computer modem, or in writing. These methods are becoming more common as technology expands.

- *Is the feedback well thought out and valid?* Consider all aspects of the situation and formulate meaningful, objective, and specific feedback.
- *What problems might my feedback create?* Ensure that your feedback does not inhibit or interfere with the employee's ability to perform.
- *Will my feedback damage the relationship?* Limit your feedback to issues that are performance related; deliver it in a manner that will not alienate the employee or put him or her on the defensive.

If, after answering any of these questions, you feel the result of your feedback will be negative, consider other options.

TYPES OF FEEDBACK

Feedback generally falls into two categories: positive (praising) and negative (criticism). Each has value in improving supervisor/employee relationships.

Giving Positive Feedback (Praise)

Feedback designed to compliment or encourage your employees falls into this category. Most employees like and need regular, positive feedback to know they are appreciated and are performing in an acceptable manner.

Positive feedback could include a simple, "It's good to see you," or specific performance feedback, such as, "I really appreciate your work on the annual sales summary report. It was well thought out and the graphs you included made your summary easy to understand." By giving detailed information about exactly what you liked, you are reinforcing a desired behavior. If you use this type of performance feedback regularly, you are likely to get similar behavior from your employees in the future. Why? Because you positively recognized their behavior and indirectly coached them on desired performance.

When giving performance feedback, remember to make it specific, telling the employee exactly what you liked. Telling an employee, "You did a good job," is not nearly as productive as spelling out exactly what was good about the job. Although your intent may be to encourage, by using vague feedback you may discourage or frustrate employees. They will not know what you liked about their performance; therefore, they will not be able to repeat it. Feedback must follow as closely behind the performance as possible. Lengthy delays before giving feedback weakens its effectiveness.

Receiving Positive Feedback

Many times you can negate the efforts of your employees or others who are trying to give you positive feedback. This happens when someone compliments you and you feel obliged to respond, "Oh, it was nothing," "This old suit . . . I've had it for years," or "Well, that's my job isn't it?" You could be shutting off valuable feedback. People eventually will feel that you do not welcome their comments and will keep them to themselves in the future. The simplest response is, "Thank you." If you need additional information or clarification of their comments, ask for it.

Giving Negative Feedback (Criticism)

Feedback in this category should also be constructive in nature, telling employees how they might improve their behavior. Comments should be given only after considering the questions outlined earlier in this section and should be given in an unemotional, objective, and specific manner.

Learning to give constructive criticism is probably one of the most difficult skills you will have to master. For one reason or another, most people are reluctant to tell others the things that need to be improved. Generally, this results from a fear of hurting feelings or not knowing how to handle potential emotional responses (crying, yelling, pouting). Remember the old adage, "If you can't say something nice, don't say anything at all"? It may sound good, but from a management perspective, it does nothing to aid your employee in improving behavior. Honest, tactful, and specific feedback does.

When giving constructive criticism, focus on what *can be* changed and don't criticize without making suggestions for improvement. Inappropriate comments would relate to (1) physical attributes (eyes, nose, ears, face, skin, size, etc.), (2) quality of clothing—unless specific expectations or guidelines were discussed before the person was hired and there are bona fide job requirements, or (3) any issues related to employment regulations, such as Equal Employment Opportunity laws (which deal with sex, race, age, religion, national origin, or disabilities).

Here is a six-step process for giving negative feedback effectively. In this illustration, the problem is tardiness:

1. *Tell the person exactly what you observed.* If possible, include quotes, facts, figures, dates, or other indisputable factors. *Example:* "You were 30 minutes late this morning. That is the second time this week you have not been here on time."

2. *Explain how you feel about the employee's actions and the impact of his or her behavior.* This approach usually causes the employee to reflect on the behavior. *Example:* "I feel that a pattern is developing and that concerns me. When you do not arrive on time, your co-workers have to cover for you in order for us to stay on schedule."

3. *Solicit feedback.* Be sincere in requesting information that will uncover the *real* reason for the tardiness. Often being late is just a symptom of the real problem. There could be family issues; drug or alcohol dependence; financial problems that prevent having adequate transportation; or a negative attitude because of a dislike for the job, peers, or you. Do not second-guess the cause; ask the employee. *Example:* "Can you help me understand why you are not getting to work on time?"

4. *Show support and solicit possible solutions.* Employees need to know you are there to assist them when needed. Even though you may have told them before, reinforce your commitment. *Example:* "Is there anything I can do that would get you here on time?" or, "I want to help you prevent a reoccurrence of this tardiness. What do you think *we* can do in the future to help you arrive on time?"

5. *Get a commitment to improve behavior.* Unless the employee has a sincere desire to change the behavior and improve performance, your efforts will be fruitless. You cannot, and should not, fix an employee's problems for him or her. Provide the tools and support the employees need to address the issues. *Example:* "Based on what we have discussed, I am confident that there will not be a repeat of this morning's tardiness. Will you promise to make a sincere effort to ensure that my trust is justified?"

6. *Reaffirm the employee's worth.* This is a final opportunity to show support and let the employee know that even though he or she made a mistake, the employee has not alienated you. *Example:* "I am glad we had a chance to discuss this issue. You are a good employee, and I would hate to see your performance rating suffer over something we can change. Thanks for all your hard work in the past."

Here are some additional examples highlighting inappropriate and appropriate ways of giving negative feedback:

Inappropriate:
    "You idiot, why can't you get these reports right?"

Appropriate:
    "The report you submitted had some errors. Let's discuss what happened and how we can improve . . ."

Inappropriate:
    "That's a stupid thing to say!"

Appropriate:
    "I'm not sure why you feel that way. Can you help me understand . . ."

Inappropriate:
    "It's such a simple task; what's your problem?"

Appropriate:
    "Let's schedule some time together so I can get some feedback on your understanding of the task."

■ **Feedback Practice**

With the suggestions presented in this chapter, practice giving feedback. Review Harold and Tom's interaction in the chapter-opening scenario. Practice giving feedback to Tom in a more appropriate fashion. Tape-record your comments to allow yourself to hear exactly what Tom would hear. If possible, have someone role-play the scenario with you.

You can also use this exercise to practice giving negative feedback to actual employees who need such feedback.

Receiving Negative Feedback

Having someone criticize you is an emotional experience, and one that often triggers the urge to dispute, debate, or retaliate. However, in order to improve your own behavior and coach your employees to do the same, you must learn to do the following:

- Listen to the feedback.
- Do not interrupt.
- Solicit verification or clarification of information you do not completely understand.
- Think objectively about what was said.
- Decide whether the comments were valid.
- Provide appropriate feedback (thank them, offer explanations, and/ or take necessary action).

ENCOURAGING FEEDBACK

The way you phrase your request for information often determines the type of feedback you receive. To get valid feedback, ask the following:

- "How would you handle this situation?"
- "In your own words, please tell me . . ."
- "Please give me some feedback on how you perceive . . ."
- "What should we do?"
- "What do you think?"
- "I'd like to hear more about your feelings on the matter. Could you give me some additional information?"

- "Can you explain why you feel that way?"
- "How do you feel about it?"
- "On a scale of 1 to 5, how would you rate . . .?"
- "Why?" (Use this one with care. In highly emotional situations, or said with the wrong vocal quality, you could provoke a confrontation. There really is no nice way to ask "Why?")

■ Expanding What You Have Learned

As we have seen, feedback is a key element in building and maintaining relationships in the workplace. Take a few minutes to reflect on some key points of this chapter by answering the following questions:

1. There are numerous reasons for communication breaking down when giving feedback. List at least three:

   _____

   _____

   _____

2. What are some of the ways you send feedback?

   _____

   _____

   _____

3. By asking yourself some questions before providing feedback, you improve your chances of success. What questions might you ask?

   _____

   _____

   _____

4. What are two common types of feedback?

   _____

   _____

   _____

5. What are the steps in the process for giving negative feedback?

   _____

   _____

   _____

6. What should you do in order to effectively receive negative feedback?

_____

_____

_____

5

Chapter 5 Checkpoints

✓ Feedback is a crucial element of communicating with others.

✓ Numerous factors contribute to the breakdown of communication. Be aware of what they are and strive to avoid them.

✓ You are constantly sending feedback messages in a variety of ways. Ensure that the messages sent are the ones you intend.

✓ Before giving feedback, consider how it might be received, and determine the best time, place, context, and format for delivery.

✓ Whether giving positive or negative feedback, select appropriate language.

✓ Practice giving negative feedback, and focus comments on behavior rather than on personal traits or things that cannot be changed.

✓ Do not automatically discount the negative feedback you receive. Consider its validity before reacting.

6 | Other-than-Average Performers

This chapter will help you to:

- Determine what motivates your employees.
- Recognize signs of negative behavior.
- Define strategies for dealing with substandard employees.
- Identify techniques to assist and reward above-average employees.

Trisha Washington is ready to pull her hair out. She supervises 13 telemarketers who sell a variety of travel-related products and services. Most of her employees show up for work on time, are pleasant and enthusiastic, and regularly meet their sales quotas. She has two employees who consistently outsell everyone by 20 to 30 percent. In the course of a normal shift, Trisha uses games, incentives, and positive coaching strategies to try to motivate employees. Still, there is one employee, Jackie Commancee, who never makes her quota. Jackie seems to be totally apathetic to Trisha's efforts and appears almost belligerent on occasion. To try to turn Jackie around, Trisha has solicited and implemented suggestions from peers and supervisors, she has observed and mentored, and she has even offered special incentives to Jackie. Nothing has worked. ■

Questions to Consider

1. What seem to be the issues in this scenario?

_____

_____

_____

2. Is Trisha taking the right approach in dealing with her employees?

_____

_____

_____

3. What else might Trisha do?

_____

_____

_____

DETERMINING EMPLOYEE NEEDS

What drives your employees and causes them to perform? According to motivation experts who have conducted studies on employees for decades, there is no one simple answer. Human behavior is very complex, and no two employees are the same. Differing backgrounds, expectations, goals, and personalities can create situations where you may be at a loss for action. With all the diversity now in the workplace, you need to be aware of changing needs. What motivated employees in the 1950s does not always work today. Employees in today's workplace are more independent, better educated, more traveled, and less likely to stay in one job their entire career. Many of today's workers also have shorter attention spans, a high desire for leisure time activities, and a desire for meaningful work. To best utilize the talents and creativity of your employees, you will need to identify their individual "hot buttons" or what inspires them.

Take a few minutes to think about your employees as a group. What factors do you believe most of them would rank as important to them? Use the following Motivator Rating Sheet to answer this question. Make copies of the sheet and rank the items on it from 1 to 14 in order of "most" to "least" important, as you feel your employees would. Once you have done this, give copies of the form to all of your employees and ask them to rank the items. Compare the sheets to verify how accurately you anticipated their needs. Keep individual responses in employees' informal files to use later in coaching and developing action plans for each person.

Motivator Rating Sheet
☐ Advancement in the organization.
☐ Secure work.

Motivator Rating Sheet
(continued)

☐ Solid benefits package.

☐ High wages.

☐ Interesting and challenging work.

☐ Fair and equitable supervisor.

☐ Safe comfortable work environment.

☐ Participation in decision making.

☐ Personal and professional development opportunities.

☐ Good work schedule.

☐ Recognition for work done.

☐ Sympathetic assistance with personal issues.

☐ Team-oriented work environment.

☐ Opportunities to have fun at work.

6

PERFORMANCE LEVEL

Once you have determined the factors that affect employee performance, use that knowledge in the coaching process model (see Chapter 3) to help address performance gaps. Since it is likely that you have employees performing below, at, and above standards, you will have to allocate your time, efforts, and resources to address each group. The following indicators of performance should be used to determine how well a given employee is doing.

Indicators of Performance

- Does the employee meet established standards and goals?

- Are there complaints from other employees about this employee?

- What are current quality and quantity levels?

- How much initiative and enthusiasm does the employee exhibit?

> **Indicators of Performance**
> **(continued)**
>
> - How well does the employee get along with fellow employees. Are customers satisfied with the employee?
> - How are the cleanliness, organization, and arrangement of the employee's work area?
> - What is the employee's current level of absenteeism, tardiness, and sick-leave usage?
> - Can the employee handle a variety of tasks?
> - Does the employee seek complex or difficult assignments?
> - Does the employee openly communicate with others?

Have you used any of these indicators to determine your employees' performance levels? What other questions do or might you ask?

DEALING WITH SUBSTANDARD PERFORMERS

Often you must deal with a lot of baggage that employees bring to the workplace because many employees cannot separate their personal problems from their jobs. Your focus should be only on performance-related issues, and you should refer employees' personal problems to human resources or other qualified sources. Some people have deeply rooted psychological problems. You have neither the time nor possibly the training to handle them. Even if you have been trained in psychological or sociological areas, you should avoid involvement because of potential legal consequences and because of the time commitment such involvement would take.

Employees fail to perform or meet standards and goals for many reasons. Generally, the causes fall into three categories:

1. They won't.
2. They can't.
3. They don't know how.

They Won't

They are not motivated.   For some reason, you and/or the job are not pushing the right "hot button" for your employees. By identifying and addressing needs, you can possibly start to turn your employees around. The easiest and surest way to discover their needs is to ask them. Do not try to second-guess or assume you know what they want.

In addition to the list of motivators provided earlier, you can determine needs by:

- *Observing employees closely*. Identify tasks they do well and regularly, as well as tasks they avoid.
- *Talking to others*. Find out if employees have expressed special interest in assignments or projects.
- *Administering personality-profile surveys*. Numerous reputable brands are on the market. Most divide personality traits or preferences into categories based on responses to a questionnaire. From the preferences identified, you can develop action plans to address the particular styles of your employees.
- *Reviewing past performance records and reports*. What have the employees done well? Which tasks did they have problems with? Are there trends?

They have a poor attitude.   A poor attitude is often evidenced by a lack of concern for work quality, low initiative, and lack of involvement. Dealing with an attitude issue takes time, patience, and a lot of one-on-one coaching. If you identify and address employees' motivation issues, as outlined earlier, and employees still fail to perform, you may have to seek guidance from your manager and possibly take disciplinary action.

They Can't

They lack the ability.   If employees cannot seem to master a task, you may have to spend extra time with them, assign a peer coach, or reassign them to a job they can perform. If their inability to perform is related to a disability, you *must* consider making reasonable accommodations to allow them to perform essential functions.

Outside factors impede them.   Many times your employees run into roadblocks because they do not have the knowledge, materials, access to you, or authority to overcome them. Some of these roadblocks relate to:

- Co-workers.
- Policies.
- Technology.
- Procedures.
- Scheduling.
- Other supervisory personnel.

Be alert to possible obstacles, show support, and help whenever possible.

Inadequate supervisory guidance.   The importance of coaching, is amplified when dealing with a poor performer. The 80/20 rule of having 80 percent of your time taken up by the 20 percent of poor performers is probably accurate. You must be careful not to neglect other employees while trying to "fix" a broken one. Provide as much support, training, and guidance as you can, but if no improvement occurs, consider disciplinary or administrative options based on your organization's policy.

They Don't Know How

Lack of technical or job knowledge.   To eliminate this issue, be sure that you follow the guidelines outlined in Chapters 2 and 4 regarding orientation, training, and coaching. Employees often get frustrated when they have inadequate knowledge or skills, yet many are reluctant to ask for assistance. This hesitancy often stems from fear of seeming incompetent or unable to do their job. It could also be an indicator that the supervisor-employee communication system has broken down. Take time to observe, evaluate, and assist employees. Provide the information, training, and tools your employees need to be successful.

Can you think of other causes of poor performance? List them here.

■ Performance Reflection

Think about three poor performers you have known (employees, co-workers, or bosses). What factors contributed to their performance deficits? What was done to deal with the problem(s)? With these questions in mind, fill in the following:

Person	Contributing Performance Factors	Action Taken
1. _____	_____	_____
2. _____	_____	_____
3. _____	_____	_____

TYPES OF POOR PERFORMERS

6

Poor performers come in many varieties. The more common types of poor performers, along with methods of dealing with them, are described below.

Type	Indicators	Possible Causes	Possible Results	Corrective Action(s)
Borderline Performer	■ Sometime reaches standard. ■ Occasional/frequent abuser of policy or procedure. ■ Knows how to manipulate the system to own advantage. ■ Abuses annual/sick leave. ■ Does not meet deadlines. ■ Fails to follow through on commitments.	■ Poor attitude. ■ Drugs/alcohol. ■ Improper corrective action in the past (reinforced negative behavior by a supervisor).	■ Lowered productivity. ■ Frustration, resentment, and lowered morale (yours and other employees). ■ Physical injury to self or others.	■ Take action immediately. ■ Use feedback process from Chapter 5. ■ Refer personal problems to trained personnel. ■ Document. ■ If necessary, terminate.

6

Type	Indicators	Possible Causes	Possible Results	Corrective Action(s)
Complaining Performer	■ Unhappy. ■ Misses deadlines. ■ Rumors of dissatisfaction. ■ Excessive time on nonwork-related conversations. ■ Undermines supervisor/policy.	■ Dissatisfaction with you, job, or co-workers. ■ Low self-esteem (easier to blame others). ■ Past experiences (it has gotten them attention in the past).	■ Lowered productivity and morale (theirs, yours, co-workers). ■ Frustration. ■ Lost revenue for organization. ■ Paying employee for work not performed.	■ Listen compassionately. ■ Create caring environment. ■ Ask questions. ■ Don't argue. ■ Solicit possible solutions and negotiate, if necessary. ■ As a last resort, tell the employee to stop or face disciplinary action. ■ Document. ■ Follow through on threats of disciplinary action, if necessary.
Plateaued Performer	■ "Retired on the job" (little initiative or enthusiasm). ■ Complacency. ■ Relaxed approach to task completion. ■ Misses deadlines.	■ Burn out. ■ Lack of challenge. ■ Blocked promotion/ professional development. ■ Lack of rewards. ■ Inadequate coaching.	■ Frustration (yours and theirs). ■ Lowered productivity. ■ Lost revenue for organization. ■ Lost talent/knowledge. ■ Increased supervisor coaching time.	■ Set and reinforce goals. ■ Coach. ■ Change work environment. ■ Job enhancement. ■ Job enrichment. ■ Incentives. ■ Cross-train. ■ Counsel, if necessary. ■ Document. ■ Take disciplinary action.
Rebellious Performer	■ Overtly or covertly undermines you and the organization. ■ Sarcasm. ■ Lack of loyalty. ■ Workplace disruptions (arguments, lack of cooperation, fights). ■ Won't perform certain tasks.	■ Deeply rooted behavior patterns. ■ Anger over something in the workplace. ■ Frustration over missed promotion or professional develop opportunity. ■ Need for attention.	■ Anger, frustration and resentment (you and co-workers). ■ Friction within workteam. ■ Lowered productivity and morale. ■ Increased supervisor coaching time. ■ Lost revenue. ■ Injury to self and/or others.	■ Coach. ■ Listen. ■ Emphasize cost to employee and the organization. ■ Patience. ■ Documentation. ■ Disciplinary action and termination if necessary.

Note: The indicators in this chart are often only symptoms of a larger and more serious problem. Investigate each situation carefully before you take action. Otherwise you may be only temporarily addressing the issue.

DEALING WITH SUPERSTARS

6

If you are like most supervisors, you have at least one employee who consistently meets or exceeds established standards or goals. A "superstar" can be both a blessing and a curse, either very helpful and productive or terribly frustrating, depending on a number of factors. Recognizing superstars is easy. They are the employees who:

- Constantly volunteer for additional assignments.
- Exceed deadlines.
- Regularly make recommendations for improvements.
- Help others.
- Work in the community.
- Test your coaching abilities and push you to stay one step ahead of them.

Sounds wonderful, doesn't it? But if their sole purpose is to make themselves look good at the expense of you and their co-workers, you have a problem. Workers like this will cause you to spend more time coaching frustrated, complaining peers. Should you have such employees on your team:

- Patiently, but firmly, guide and coach them.
- Harness their capabilities by appealing to their egos.
- Use them in positions of authority (peer coaches, team/committee leaders).
- Give them lots of praise (privately and publicly).

Should they fail to contribute positively, you should document efforts, counsel, and discipline as you would with any problem employee. Often, if superstars perceive you as an ally, mentor, or champion of their cause, they will enhance rather than complicate your role as supervisor.

Think about your subordinates. Do you have any superstars? What are some ways you currently use their talents? How else might you use them in the future?

Many high achievers expect acknowledgment of their accomplishments. Here are some ideas for rewarding their performance and addressing their needs. Not everyone responds to the same motivators; therefore, ask your employees what they would like.

- Put them in leadership positions (team leaders, coordinators, project managers, committee chairs).
- Expand their job responsibilities.
- Use them as peer coaches, trainers, or internal consultants.
- Praise them regularly and openly.
- Solicit their advice.
- Involve them in decision making.
- Provide personal and professional development opportunities.
- Support their involvement in professional/civic organizations.
- Encourage them and provide opportunities for advancement.
- Position them in highly visible positions (customer contact, committees).

Expanding What You Have Learned

1. What value does determining employee needs serve?

_____

_____

2. In your workplace, what could contribute to substandard employee performance?

_____

_____

3. What can you do to change number 2?

_____

_____

4. Of the types of employees identified in this chapter, which do you have the most trouble dealing with? Why?

_____

_____

5. What resources do you have available to deal with other-than-average employees?

_____

_____

6

Chapter 6 Checkpoints

✓ Never assume you know what motivates people; ask them.

✓ Develop strategies for dealing with above- and below-average employees.

✓ Whether substandard employees can't, won't, or don't know how to perform their jobs, it is your job to help them.

✓ There are many telltale indicators of performance. Be alert for them.

7 | Coaching Performers with Special Needs

This chapter will help you to:

- Identify key employment issues of the Americans with Disabilities Act (ADA) and their impact on your coaching of employees.

- Recognize your responsibilities under the ADA.

- Explore strategies for establishing a work environment that includes persons with disabilities.

- Provide appropriate support and guidance to employees with disabilities.

- Productively integrate employees with disabilities into your work team.

Vinny Delgado was a bit anxious. He had been interviewing candidates for an open food-server position in the food services department for over a week. He received a call from the human resources recruiter informing him that he was to interview an applicant with an arm prosthesis. His immediate reaction was amazement. He wondered how such a person could possibly carry food inserts, arrange furnishings, and handle the daily tasks in a cafeteria environment. Vinny was not sure what kinds of questions he could ask the applicant. Wasn't there some statute that covered this sort of thing?

Upon meeting the applicant, Joel Murdock, Vinny was struck by his openness and affable nature. After looking over Joel's resume and hearing of over six years' experience in food service facilities, Vinny decided to hire him. The issue of Joel's disability was never actually discussed. During the interview, Vinny did learn that for the past two years Joel had successfully performed many different tasks in a full-service restaurant, including filling in for the supervisor when she was out of the restaurant. ■

Questions to Consider

1. How do you feel about Vinny's initial reaction to interviewing a person with a disability? Why?

_____

_____

_____

2. Do you think Joel will be successful in the new job? Explain.

_____

_____

_____

3. Could Vinny have done anything to better prepare for this interview with Joel? Were there any questions that Vinny would have been prohibited from asking Joel?

_____

_____

_____

4. Does Vinny's organization have an obligation to assist Joel perform the essential functions of the job if such assistance should become necessary? Why or why not?

_____

_____

_____

ASSESS YOUR KNOWLEDGE

Until recently, many supervisors and organizations have excluded a huge untapped reservoir of potential employees from serious consideration. Specifically, one-sixth of the population of the United States has been virtually ignored. Who makes up this massive gold mine of human resources? People with disabilities. Fortunately, new legislation has begun to change the way people with disabilities are treated. The Americans with Disabilities Act (ADA) **requires** you and your organization to consider qualified applicants with disabilities just as you would consider qualified nondisabled applicants. Because of the far-reaching implications of this law, it has been called the most sweeping piece of civil rights legislation to be enacted since the 1964 Civil Rights Act. In this chapter, we will focus on your responsibilities under the ADA's employment section.

Before going further, test your knowledge of the provisions of the ADA by completing the following quiz. Circle T for true or F for false. Answers appear on page 78:

T F **1.** The Americans with Disabilities Act of 1990 provides protection to an estimated 43 million people.

T F **2.** Under the ADA, an alcoholic who has been rehabilitated is protected in employment-related situations.

T F **3.** The mother and sole provider of a child with Down's syndrome has guaranteed rights under the ADA.

T F **4.** Reasonable accommodation costs can be used to disqualify a potential job applicant.

T F **5.** An employee who becomes disabled in an automobile accident must be accommodated under the ADA.

T F **6.** According to Title I of the ADA, employers must have a current job description in place for each position in their organization.

T F **7.** Preexisting conditions can be used to deny health insurance under the ADA.

T F **8.** Obesity that precludes the performance of the essential functions of a job may be included as a protected status under the ADA.

T F **9.** *Handicap* is the preferred term for someone with a disabling condition.

T F **10.** Federal funds are available to assist employers with the costs of accommodation for employees with disabilities.

7

> ■ **Hints** ──────────────────────────────
>
> ### Americans with Disabilities Act Facts
>
> - The ADA was signed into law on July 26, 1990.
> - The ADA provides protection to an estimated 43 million Americans.
> - An estimated 750,000 Americans with disabilities will enter the work force each year.
> - On July 26, 1992, organizations with 25 or more employees are affected by the ADA.
> - On July 26, 1994, organizations with 15 or more employees are affected by the ADA.
> - Five major categories are covered by the ADA:
>   Title I: Employment
>   Title II: Public service and transportation
>   Title III: Public accommodations
>   Title IV: Telecommunications
>   Title V: Other provisions
> - The Equal Employment Opportunity Commission (EEOC) is responsible for enforcement of the ADA.
> - There is no affirmative action requirement under the ADA.
> - Specific guidance and definitions are available from the EEOC's technical assistance manuals.

ESTABLISHING A NONTHREATENING WORKPLACE

The Americans with Disabilities Act opens employment opportunities traditionally closed to people with disabilities. It is expected that larger percentages of the workforce will have disabilities in the future. If your organization does not have a formal ADA awareness program, it should. This would facilitate open communication and harmonious interactions among all workers.

A key strategy to implement immediately is to educate your staff about the ADA and what it means. Raise their awareness of the capabilities of people with disabilities and work toward developing an atmosphere that fosters inclusiveness. You can start by examining your own vocabulary related to people with disabilities. When referring to employees with disabilities, always refer to the person first, then the disability. *Example: John uses a wheelchair.*

Instead of ————————→	Use
"John is a victim of . . ."	"John has . . ."
"Sue is afflicted with . . ."	"Sue has . . ."
"Jim is confined to a wheelchair."	"Jim has a mobility impairment" or "Jim uses a wheelchair."
"Handicapped"	"Disabled" or "Physically or mentally challenged"
"Suffering from . . ."	". . . has . . ."
"Deaf and dumb"	"Has a hearing and speaking disability"
"Joan is an epileptic."	"Joan has epilepsy."

Think about other terminology you and your co-workers currently use that could be considered offensive. Write it down here and make a concerted effort to end its use.

STRATEGIES FOR SUCCESS

To help in developing an inclusive workplace, consider these tips:

- Read and research the ADA. Read up on various types of disabilities. Hundreds of books and articles are on the market that address the ADA and people with disabilities. Read as many as possible and pass the information on to your employees.

- Have experts from local disability advocacy groups come in to speak with your employees about disabilities.

- Work with your human resources department to make reasonable accommodations for new or current employees.

- Ensure that applicants and employees with disabilities have equal access to all workplace opportunities available to nondisabled employees.
- Provide sensitivity training on dealing with people who have disabilities, just as you address other diversity issues through training.
- Work with all employees to dispel myths about people with disabilities.

MYTHS ABOUT PEOPLE WITH DISABILITIES

Myths normally result from fears, negative stereotypes, or ignorance. Generally, these are the products of early experiences related to disabilities. Children are often told "not to stare," "just ignore them," or "don't ask," when a person with a disability is encountered. It is no wonder that the following myths exist:

- *Using a wheelchair is confining.* Not true. In fact, most users of wheelchairs think of them the same way a car is viewed, as devices that aid mobility.
- *Supervising people with disabilities is hard work.* True, but it is no harder than supervising nondisabled workers. If you have a system in place for coaching employees, it should be no harder to supervise employees with disabilities than to supervise nondisabled employees. Employees with disabilities do face challenges, but so do all employees.
- *People with disabilities live with tragedy and frustration.* Not true. Persons with disabilities live fulfilling lives with laughing, crying, ups, and downs—like anyone else.
- *Employees with disabilities will cause workers' compensation rates to rise. They are accident prone.* Not true. According to a 1990 joint DuPont/U.S. Department of Labor study, 97 percent of employees with disabilities ranked average or above on safety issues.
- *Absenteeism and turnover are higher for employees with disabilities.* Not true. In studies conducted by the U.S. Department of Vocational Rehabilitation, 95 percent of employees with disabilities ranked as well as, or better than, nondisabled employees in absenteeism, and 99 percent ranked as well as or better in turnover.

DAY-TO-DAY SUPERVISION

The ADA does not require that you lower job standards or give special treatment or consideration to employees with disabilities. In fact, most people with disabilities do not want special treatment. What they want, and what the law requires, is an equal opportunity to perform their jobs and earn a living. When supervising employees with disabilities, provide the same attention that you do to other employees. Coach, guide, mentor, and appraise performance. If they perform well, reward them. If they make mistakes, coach them. If they perform poorly or violate policy, discipline them—just as you would other employees. The following are a few considerations to keep in mind:

1. *Coach regularly.* Depending on your reason for coaching, you may have to modify your approach in order to be effective.

2. *Ensure that training materials, activities, facilities, and instructions are accessible to employees with disabilities.* Your training or human resources department may be able to help. If you do not have access to these departments, contact the American Society for Training and

Development at 1640 King Street, Box 1443, Alexandria, Virginia 22313–2043. It has numerous excellent publications available on training employees with disabilities. In addition, the publishers of this book offer *The Americans with Disabilities Act: What Supervisors Need to Know.*

3. *Adapt your one-on-one coaching technique.* Certain disabilities may require you to think of how to present instruction. An example would be an employee with a learning disability. He or she may require added patience and repeated demonstration of a technique. This approach is really no different from those you would take with nondisabled employees.

4. *Give effective feedback.* Realize that in many instances some employees with disabilities have little or no previous work experience. Use the coaching process model and suggestions given in Chapter 5 as guides.

5. *Provide professional development opportunities.* Help employees with disabilities prepare for increased responsibility and promotion. Provide job enrichment and job enhancement opportunities.

6. *Determine necessary accommodations.* Work with the employee to determine what method, process, or equipment can be implemented to allow the employee to perform his or her job and meet standards.

7. *Assign a peer coach.* Ensure that the peer helps provide a warm, open environment for the employee with a disability. Remind the peer coach to assist in encouraging other employees to help provide friendly interaction. Also, before allowing the peer to coach employees with disabilities, provide sensitivity/diversity awareness training to ensure that the peer feels comfortable in his or her role and has the knowledge to provide a supportive relationship.

Expanding What You Have Learned

1. The intent of the ADA is to promote equal opportunities for employees with disabilities and to destroy stereotypical job assignments. What types of jobs are employees with disabilities performing in your organization? Do they have *equal* access to job opportunities?

   _____

   _____

   _____

2. What are some things you can do to help eliminate concerns and apprehensions about working with employees with disabilities?

---

3. You have read several suggestions for including employees with disabilities. What other actions can you take to ensure inclusiveness in work and social settings?

7

▌ ADA Quiz Answers

1. **True**. There are an estimated 43 million Americans with disabilities. It is estimated that 750,000 people with disabilities will enter the workplace each year.

2. **True**. People currently using and abusing alcohol or drugs are not protected. However, recovering alcoholics and addicts are.

3. **True**. Under the Americans with Disabilities Act, it is "unlawful to discriminate against qualified individuals because of the known disability of a person with whom the individual has a relationship or an association."

4. **False**. No dollar amount is used in the Americans with Disabilities Act to define "reasonable accommodation." The law states that "otherwise qualified" individuals must be given equal access to job opportunities and that reasonable accommodations must be made.

5. **True**. The Americans with Disabilities Act covers all persons with disabilities, not just job applicants.

6. **False**. Although the Americans with Disabilities Act does not require a written job description, it is a good idea to have one in place. This will assist interviewers in hiring the best possible applicant, and it could prove useful in protecting against potential litigation.

7. **True**. Noncoverage of preexisting conditions may be included in health-care policies, as long as it is not added as a way to circumvent the provisions of the ADA.

8. **True**. Although obesity is not considered a disability under the Americans with Disabilities Act, if it inhibits an individual's major life functions and prevents the individual from performing an essential job function, it could be covered.

9. **False**. The term *handicapped* is derived from an Old English reference to "cap in hand," or beggar. Because of the negative connotation associated with the term, preferred terminology is *disabled*, or *person with a disability*.

10. **True**. Numerous federal and state agencies, as well as a host of advocacy groups, can be contacted to assist in accommodating individuals with disabilities. Funding and tax breaks are only a few of the options available to employers who hire employees with disabilities.

Chapter 7 Checkpoints

✓ Identify and eliminate negative stereotypes and myths about employees with disabilities.

✓ Familiarize your employees with the requirements of the ADA.

✓ Work to establish a nonthreatening environment.

✓ Search your vocabulary and discard potentially offensive or inappropriate words for referring to employees with disabilities.

✓ Plan a strategy for success.

✓ Develop an action plan to coach, guide, and supervise all employees.

8 | Coaching Documentation

This chapter will help you to: ─────────

- Recognize the need for the maintenance of performance documentation.
- Establish a system for tracking employee performance.
- Develop objective documentation of performance.

Mary Ann Roberts joined Custom Drapes, Inc., as a supervisor one and a half months ago. She is the third supervisor in the position in the past year. The first supervisor resigned, and the second was promoted and transferred to another state after only three months on the job.

Mary Ann arrived in the middle of the store's busiest season and has had little time to get settled in or coach her employees. Normally, she prefers to have established systems in place and to maintain ongoing communication with her employees. She also likes to maintain an informal performance file on each person during the year. Unfortunately, she has been able to do none of this yet. To compound her situation, Mary Ann just discovered that one of her employees, Dana McGregor, has a performance appraisal due next week. At this point Mary Ann has no documentation on the employee and is frustrated. ■

Questions to Consider
1. What are some problems in this scenario?

_____

_____

_____

2. How do you think Mary Ann will do in evaluating Dana's performance? Explain.

_____

_____

_____

3. What can Mary Ann do at this point to ensure that Dana gets a fair evaluation?

_____

_____

_____

WHY DOCUMENT?

The importance of developing, maintaining, and referring to performance documentation on an employee should never be underestimated. While it is easier to avoid documenting, it is not prudent to do so. Documentation serves many purposes and provides numerous benefits. Some of the benefits are as follows:

- _It provides a chronological record of performance._ Regular entries made throughout the performance period display a step-by-step picture of how the employee has performed over a given period of time.

- _It aids in the recall of information._ Performance information is often needed but difficult to recall, especially if you have several employees. Documentation reduces the loss of important examples of an employee's performance.

- _It serves as a reference._ When an employee or supervisor is promoted or transferred to another location, the documentation aids the new supervisor with an objective overview of the employee's performance up to that point.

- _It furnishes specific examples of performance._ These can be used to justify ratings on performance appraisals and in court. By coaching and documenting throughout the performance appraisal period, you avoid surprises at the performance appraisal interview. You simply transfer your coaching comments from the informal file and review overall performance with the employee.

- *It makes your job easier.* By providing a tracking mechanism for employee performance, you have to do less collecting and recollecting of information when you need it.

SOURCES OF PERFORMANCE INFORMATION

Data on employee performance is available from a variety of sources. All are valuable in creating a clear picture of the type of worker you have and his or her capabilities, accomplishments, and areas for improvement. Sources of performance information include:

- Previous employee performance appraisal forms.
- Other supervisors or employees who have knowledge of the employee's work patterns.
- Reports.
- Letters of appreciation and reprimand.
- Certificates of completion and attendance.
- Written performance goals.
- Job descriptions.
- Attendance records.

8

ESTABLISHING THE DOCUMENTATION SYSTEM

Every supervisor should maintain an informal file on each employee. It can serve as a record of coaching sessions and other significant performance events. It also can serve as a memory jogger and a prime source of information in cases of disciplinary action against a poor performer.

Whenever a new employee joins your team, you should establish a file and begin documenting behavior. Your first entry should be the date that he or she joined your team and an outline of what was covered in the orientation. By starting on the first day, you begin a routine and do not miss important data. This comes in handy in cases where the employee claims he or she did not receive certain initial information.

It is important that you inform employees during orientation of your system for tracking performance. Otherwise, they may think you are trying to hide something or "get them." By informing them of the file and readily showing the contents, you build trust and encourage dialogue. It is also a good idea to have employees keep their own performance file. Before the performance appraisal, you can compare notes for accuracy.

Format

Setting up an informal file system is relatively easy. Take a file folder, punch two holes at the top of both sides, and put in a clip to secure the papers. Next put one copy of the Performance Tracking Sheet (Satisfactory) on the left side and one (Areas for Improvement) on the right side. The forms can be as simple as the sample ones below.

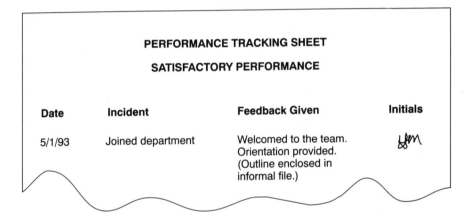

PERFORMANCE TRACKING SHEET

SATISFACTORY PERFORMANCE

Date	Incident	Feedback Given	Initials
5/1/93	Joined department	Welcomed to the team. Orientation provided. (Outline enclosed in informal file.)	

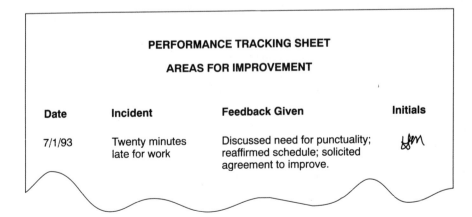

PERFORMANCE TRACKING SHEET

AREAS FOR IMPROVEMENT

Date	Incident	Feedback Given	Initials
7/1/93	Twenty minutes late for work	Discussed need for punctuality; reaffirmed schedule; solicited agreement to improve.	

As the performance period progresses, simply add additional sheets. Any miscellaneous documentation gathered (letters, certificates, or whatever) are stored in the folder with a notation made on the appropriate tracking sheet.

Considerations

Strive to make your documentation as specific and complete as possible. It is better to have too much information than not enough. When filing information in an employee's file:

- *Maintain a neat and orderly file.* This sends a message of your professionalism to others who view the file.

- *Record data clearly and concisely.* When you are ready to use the information, you will have a graphic picture of the employee's performance.

- *Remain objective.* Use measurable criteria to explain behavior (times, dates, quotes, quantity, or quality of achievements). Avoid biases, opinions, or misleading information.

- *Avoid contradictions.* Ensure that you do not have data that contradicts previous entries. This could destroy credibility or confuse others reading the file.

8

- *Stay focused on job performance.* There should be no entries related to the employee's personal life. Nor should there be any opinions as to why the employee performed in a certain manner.
- *Ensure thoroughness.* Make sure that you have all the supporting data or documentation needed to substantiate entries.
- *Date and initial (or sign) all entries.* This provides a chronology of progressive performance and lets others know who made the observations.

WHY SOME SUPERVISORS DON'T DOCUMENT

You could join thousands of other supervisors in the business world who do not document employee performance. Or you could make your job easier while becoming more effective and efficient. Just as with coaching, the time you spend documenting pays off later. Here are some excuses why some supervisors do not document, along with reasons for overcoming them:

- **"I don't have time."** The effort used to document after each coaching session or performance activity is minimal compared to the time involved in going back to reconstruct a record at performance appraisal time.
- **"I forgot."** If you start documenting performance of your employees today and do it everyday, it will become a habit. To establish a pattern to avoid forgetting, set aside 30 to 60 minutes each Friday to enter data.
- **"I don't know how."** Documentation is nothing more than writing down what you observed and discussed with the employee. Anyone can do it.
- **"It's not required."** Documentation may not be required, but it certainly makes your job easier.
- **"It can be used as evidence against me in court."** Although it is true that documentation could be obtained during the discovery process of a trial, if you follow the suggestions under the documentation considerations section earlier, you should not be afraid of this occurrence.

■ Expanding What You Have Learned

1. What are some of the benefits to documenting employee performance?

_____

_____

_____

2. In addition to your personal observation of the employee's performance, what are some sources of performance information?

_____

_____

_____

3. What are the basic elements that your documentation should include?

_____

_____

_____

4. The format of your documentation system is not important; however, there are several things to consider when documenting. What are some of these considerations?

_____

_____

_____

8

Chapter 8 Checkpoints

✓ Document examples of employee performance regularly.

✓ Follow a consistent format for documenting performance.

✓ Avoid excuses for not documenting.

✓ Ensure that your documentation provides an accurate and complete picture of the employee's performance.

✓ Keep in mind all the benefits of documentation.

✓ As soon as a new employee starts, establish a documentation file for that employee.

Post-Test

Now that you have completed the material in this book, take a few minutes to test your understanding of key coaching concepts. Once you have completed the test, check your answers. Review any material related to questions with which you have difficulty. Circle T for true or F for false.

T F   **1.** An effective way to coach employees during a project is to add additional details pertaining to the next phase as they complete the one they are currently working on. This prevents confusion.

T F   **2.** To ensure that all employees are successful in their individual roles, an effective leader will always strive to provide win-win situations.

T F   **3.** The best coaches are concerned with employees' personal as well as professional development.

T F   **4.** Immediate, nonspecific performance feedback fuels a winning team.

T F   **5.** Employees need measurable, attainable goals in order to reach their fullest potential.

T F   **6.** Successful coaches solicit, listen to, and take action on employee suggestions.

T F   **7.** It is not really necessary to explain to employees why decisions are made.

T F   **8.** High returns are attained by employees who are encouraged to be creative and proactive.

T F   **9.** The same rewards should be provided to all employees for their performance in order to prevent jealousy.

T   F   **10.** When giving constructive criticism, suggested improvements along with positive feedback concerning the employee's abilities should be discussed.

Business Skills Express Series

This growing series of books addresses a broad range of key business skills and topics to meet the needs of employees, human resource departments, and training consultants.

To obtain information about these and other Business Skills Express books, please contact the Director of Special Sales, McGraw-Hill, 11 West 19th Street, New York, NY 10011.

Effective Performance Management
ISBN 1-55623-867-3

Hiring the Best
ISBN 1-55623-865-7

Writing that Works
ISBN 1-55623-856-8

Customer Service Excellence
ISBN 1-55623-969-6

Writing for Business Results
ISBN 1-55623-854-1

Powerful Presentation Skills
ISBN 1-55623-870-3

Meetings that Work
ISBN 1-55623-866-5

Effective Teamwork
ISBN 1-55623-880-0

Time Management
ISBN 1-55623-888-6

Assertiveness Skills
ISBN 1-55623-857-6

Motivation at Work
ISBN 1-55623-868-1

Overcoming Anxiety at Work
ISBN 1-55623-869-X

Positive Politics at Work
ISBN 1-55623-879-7

Telephone Skills at Work
ISBN 1-55623-858-4

Managing Conflict at Work
ISBN 1-55623-890-8

The New Supervisor: Skills for Success
ISBN 1-55623-762-6

The *Americans with Disabilities Act*: What Supervisors Need to Know
ISBN 1-55623-889-4

Managing the Demands of Work and Home
ISBN 0-7863-0221-6

Effective Listening Skills
ISBN 0-7863-0122-8

Goal Management at Work
ISBN 0-7863-0225-9

Positive Attitudes at Work
ISBN 0-7863-0167-8

Supervising the Difficult Employee
ISBN 0-7863-0219-4

Cultural Diversity in the Workplace
ISBN 0-7863-0125-2

Managing Organizational Change
ISBN 0-7863-0162-7

Negotiating for Business Results
ISBN 0-7863-0114-7

Practical Business Communication
ISBN 0-7863-0227-5

High Performance Speaking
ISBN 0-7863-0222-4

Delegation Skills
ISBN 0-7863-0148-1

Coaching Skills: A Guide for Supervisors
ISBN 0-7863-0220-8

Customer Service and the Telephone
ISBN 0-7863-0224-0

Creativity at Work
ISBN   0-7863-0223-2

Effective Interpersonal Relationships
ISBN   0-7863-0255-0

The Participative Leader
ISBN   0-7863-0252-6

Building Customer Loyalty
ISBN   0-7863-0253-4

Getting and Staying Organized
ISBN   0-7863-0254-2

Multicultural Customer Service
ISBN   0-7863-0332-8

Business Etiquette
ISBN   0-7863-0323-9

Empowering Employees
ISBN   0-7863-0314-X

Training Skills for Supervisors
ISBN   0-7863-0313-1

Moving Meetings
ISBN   0-7863-0333-6